The Art of Emptiness

Purifying Your Space to Free Your Soul

Carolyn L. Hetzel

Revised and Corrected Edition

Contents

"Perfection is achieved, not when there is nothing more to add, but when there is nothing left to take away" - *Antoine de Saint-Exupéry*

Introduction: Declutter Your Life!

"Simplicity is the essence of happiness." - *Cedric Bledsoe*

We live in excess. Too many possessions, too many TV channels, too much food, too many contacts, too much leisure, too many choices, too much of everything. For most of us, however, this way of living no longer suits us.

We no longer want to run around senselessly, without ever questioning or remembering why. We no longer want that adulterated food, those ready-made but tasteless dishes, prepared without love, packed with fats, salt, sugar, and long-term harmful chemicals. We no longer want to be lobotomized constantly by screens of all sizes that rehash the same sorted and filtered information over and over. We no longer want to be chained to our mobile phones or social networks.

Perhaps this explains the current demand for a return to simplicity, decluttering, to the natural. We want to live with less, but better. We want to live at our own pace, a normal pace, that is, in harmony with the universe, with those around us, with the needs of our body. We need to rediscover the taste for life, for simple things, for contact with nature. How long has it been since you last walked barefoot in the grass?

The asphalt, the artificial, the fake cut us off from our natural source of energy: the Earth. The media and digital bombardment, the overload of mental solicitations cut us off from our source of inspiration and our connection with our true identity: our soul.

If you, too, are tired of living this senseless life, this race for consumption, if you feel caught in a web others have woven for you, then this book is for you.

And I have some very good news for you: it's never too late to change everything. But the most significant change must first occur in a place that belongs only to you: within yourself. It's in your mind that the change must first take place. It's your perception that will allow you to change.

The little book you are about to read does not claim to cover the subject exhaustively. Its purpose is essentially practical. However, a more theoretical first part will allow you to approach taking action with serenity. It lays the foundations of the minimalist spirit.

I invite you to implement the few simple steps mentioned later on. If you're reading this book, it's because you're already ready to live a different life, simpler and in fact richer. So don't wait to take action. Your new behavior will impress and influence those around you, and there's no doubt that you will quickly find new followers of this lifestyle.

By doing so, you are working not only for yourself but also for the entire planet. A new generation of consumers is emerging, more responsible, more concerned about what they leave behind, more aware of their true needs. You will soon be proud to say, along with everyone who already subscribes to this philosophy, that you are part of it.

This new world will be built with you. Welcome.

Part 1: A Bit of Theory...

Theory is to practice what roots are to a tree: the base, the foundations. It will allow you not only to understand the why and the how but will also give you the motivation necessary to take action. Moreover, a deep understanding of what minimalism is and what it entails will serve as a guide in times of doubt. You will be less susceptible to influence, whether from friends, family, or what society considers normal. Having grasped the ins and outs of your approach, you will reap the benefits more quickly. The good news is, there are many benefits, and they are waiting for you.

So, without further ado, let's embark on this journey together.

"The secret of happiness, you see, is not found in seeking more, but in developing the capacity to enjoy less." - *Socrates*

I remember a time – not so distant yet it feels so far away! – when I should have been swimming in happiness and bliss. Indeed, if we stick to what advertisers and merchants of illusion of all kinds tell us, I had a multitude of things. To be honest, I had *too much* of everything: too many books, CDs, and DVDs on the shelves of my libraries, too much crockery and utensils in my cupboards, too many knick-knacks and frames on my sideboard, too many clothes and shoes in my wardrobe, too many skincare creams, too many cleaning products, too much household linen, too much of this, too much of that, too much, too much, too much...

However, for me, it didn't work. All this clutter was draining my energy. All these trinkets were swallowing my finances as surely as a whirlpool swallows the boats passing in its wake. In short, all these material things polluted my field of vision and ultimately did not bring me anything, but moreover, deprived me of my joy of living and my creativity.

Yet, "more is better," that's what we're constantly being told, right? "More, faster, stronger"...

I realized that all this "more," not only did I not *need* it, but I also did not *want* it at all. In short, it was as if imposed on me by others, by habits and societal norms, by received ideas and family legacy. In reality, *I didn't want it.* But I had never really thought about it myself.

So, I changed everything.

While until then my possessions had continued to increase year after year, something I had considered normal and of which I was even rather proud, I decided to reverse the trend.

I started *not buying anything*. The phrase sounds odd, but it matches what I began to experience.

On the contrary, I started emptying, decluttering, throwing away, giving away, selling, day after day, over and over, until there was nothing left to remove, keeping only the essentials—what was useful and/or brought me joy (we'll come back to this)—and this process acted as a trigger. It was like a revelation, leading me well beyond mere physical decluttering.

Indeed, I discovered the *joy of giving*, whether to organizations or to acquaintances, bags of stuff I no longer wanted and that would be beneficial to them. And for what could not be given away, the simple pleasure of throwing away and **seeing emptiness replace the objects**. I discovered a sense of lightness and freedom generated by the act of emptying my shelves, my cupboards, my floor, and my furniture—and this I had not anticipated.

Initially, I never would have thought that creating emptiness could act as therapy. To be honest, I was a bit stressed, fearing that I would part with things in vain. But it was the opposite. And so, like so many others, men and women around the world, a new "minimalist" was born. I became convinced *through direct experience* that owning less indeed made me less stressed and happier.

Now that I had discovered and experienced this myself, I was so excited about this realization that I looked for ways to share it by all means possible. I started talking about it to those around me. I wanted to wake up every person I met, to shout from the rooftops that happiness is not found in overconsumption or even in consumption but rather in simplicity and returning to the essentials. Alas, or fortunately, being rather reserved by nature, I simply decided to write it down.

And so, the book that you hold in your hands was born.

I will strive here to share my thoughts in this field, not only from a practical point of view, of course—so that you too can apply this lifestyle and enjoy the many benefits it brings—but also from a philosophical perspective, because successful implementation is merely the realization of a clear vision.

You will see that on this path, even if it seems new, you will not be alone, and some illustrious names (as the quotes will remind you) will accompany you along the way.

Minimalism can even sometimes lead us to poetic impulses about things as simple as the number—necessarily sufficient—of our possessions. One only needs to read the haikus, those short Japanese poems that express so much in just three lines.

I wish for you to know the same small joys that I have experienced on this journey. I almost envy you for being at the beginning, for I know all the joys that you will encounter at each step. Once you reach the end, you will see that the result will exceed all your expectations.

Living with Less: A Philosophy

"A good traveler has no fixed plans and is not intent on arriving." - *Lao Tzu*

To rid ourselves of what clutters our life is not to make a sacrifice. It's to exchange the unnecessary and the superfluous for the essential. It's to apply an aesthetic and philosophical conception to all areas of our life. It's to protect our living space and refuse to let it be polluted, both externally and internally. It's to contribute to a cleaner world and not to add to the exploitation of our planet's resources by a frenzied race to consume useless products.

The foundation of this lifestyle is primarily based on a philosophical approach. In reality, your current lifestyle is too. The difference is that in the latter case, you adhere to a conception dictated by the current society, which sees you first and foremost as a potential consumer. In the minimalist approach, you choose to go against the grain of this vision. This entails some challenges but also great satisfactions on several levels.

In addition to a cleaner, more uncluttered interior that is easier to maintain, brighter, and more harmonious, you concretely develop and manifest your independence and will, qualities that will be useful to you for all the challenges life presents. **You** know what you want and why you want it. **You** decide what happiness means to you.

Your new philosophy allows you to feel **free**. You're no longer in the competition for who has the biggest car or the latest high-tech gadget. You're no longer chained to fashion trends, to the new style of pants everyone must wear to stay relevant, or to the latest model of sneakers that everyone is supposed to don.

In summary, your priority is no longer material possessions. You move to a different level, and a new world of possibilities opens up to you.

You gently shift towards non-attachment, and towards a more spiritual life. Your simple and frugal lifestyle reminds you that we are just passing through on Earth and that nothing we seem to own truly belongs to us.

That doesn't mean you enjoy earthly pleasures any less during your time here, quite the opposite! It's by focusing on what truly matters that you thrive.

Ultimately, it is through this means that you find and understand yourself.

Human relationships, mutual aid, creativity in all its forms become your priorities. You trade isolation for openness. The consumption of prepackaged entertainment gives way to the development of your talents and gifts.

You are free to move if you wish, to change your life without having to manage all those so-called possessions, which are in fact the source of your troubles as they keep you in the status quo through the fear of losing them.

You learn to appreciate every item you own. And you don't forget the most important part: you're just borrowing it, for a short while.

Why Become a Minimalist?

"Less is more." - *Ludwig Mies van der Rohe*

The terms *minimalism* and *minimalist* are generally still quite unknown. When they are known, they are often associated with asceticism and renunciation, with a bland and cold way of life. The slightly more curious and open-minded people ask you about the reasons that drive you to live (*"voluntarily?"* and that's when their eyes widen) in a place made of space rather than objects.

In summary, you are seen at best as an eccentric, at worst as someone boring.

However, these superficial and simplistic analyses miss the essence, the number one reason that drives us and keeps us on this path: the joy, the happiness that such a lifestyle brings. It may seem incredible and even paradoxical at first glance: how can the absence of something make us happier than its presence?

Therefore, before delving deeper into the heart of the matter, I have listed below some practical and philosophical arguments that should shed some light. These are essentially qualities and states that we tend to neglect these days and that practicing a minimalist lifestyle naturally tends to return to us.

Freedom: Owning material goods is not inherently bad, but whether we like it or not, it *binds* us: we then need a place to store them (usually a dwelling) and a source of income to buy and maintain them. This consequently restricts you in terms of mobility, and thus freedom. Without all that, you would be much more open to what life can offer you – anywhere in the world and overnight.

Ingenuity: In our relatively assisted world, we tend to overlook it, but most of the time, we can get by with what we have to accomplish most tasks we need to complete. There's no need to buy a dedicated device for every need we encounter; a minimum of creativity does the job very well.

Serenity: While lacking the vital elements necessary to satisfy our primary needs is obviously a source of stress, having too much of what we don't really need is just as stressful. To possess is to first buy, then store, maintain, clean, repair, insure... and then to get rid of, which (as you'll see) is no small feat!

Following the previous point, its little sister **peace of mind**: how nice it is not to spend one's free time cleaning, dusting, polishing, making shine a multitude of mostly unnecessary objects! And yet, when we are alone, we can put it off (which generates extra work for later), but who among you hasn't made up any excuse to avoid having someone over unexpectedly because of aggravated disorder?

Savings: Alright, it's not a quality, but isn't it better to spend your money on *living* activities (traveling, dining out with friends, seeing concerts...) than on objects that will only collect dust in addition to taking up space, in short, on *dead* things?

Mastery of one's time: It may seem trivial, but the simple process of purchasing takes a lot of time. Going to the store can easily cost you half a day, the time it takes to take your vehicle, park, make your choice, check out, possibly manage the children, maybe refuel, return, unload and store everything... Not to mention the money and energy a large store can take from you, especially on Saturday, which is the only free time slot for most people. If you shop online, it almost takes you more time! Who hasn't been surprised to realize the hours they had just spent in front of their screen? Between advertising solicitations, emails, social networks, comparison sites... Then, of course, comes the time dedicated to everything that follows, but you know this part: maintenance, repairs...

Independence: Most people are primarily *consumers*. Unfortunately, that's how society first views each of us. Being minimalist—and proclaiming it loudly—frees you from what is expected of an average consumer: to be at the cutting edge of technology, to own the latest fashion item, to have read the latest bestseller... In fact, suddenly, you benefit from the leniency of those who know you well. The opinion of those outside this circle, you'll agree, matters little.

Availability: Being less focused on material things means being more open to what is *alive*, to sharing, to others, to a cause that is dear to us. It's selling a few books we no longer read to treat oneself and others to a nice meal out. It's being present to life as it comes.

Generosity and **ecological awareness**: Consuming less means reducing our contribution to the depletion of our planet's resources and considering the fair distribution of those resources. It's trading a self-centered awareness for a planetary consciousness.

Feel free to add to this list with your own arguments. There are many, and they will motivate you in times of doubt.

Time, Space, Silence, and Shakespeare

"Everything should be made as simple as possible, but not simpler." - *Albert Einstein*

The first three elements forming the title of this paragraph are closely linked. From a spiritual point of view, they are one. If we elevate our vision further, **everything is one**. But this goes beyond the scope of our book.

However, it's appropriate to explore the correlation between these different concepts to better grasp what concerns us here.

Their commonality is this: they are zones of potentiality, blank slates that underlie and allow the existence of everything we perceive.

Silence allows for sound. Space allows for matter. Time allows for evolution. These are three forms of unfolding. Silence, space, and time have the interesting characteristic of *being and not being* simultaneously, no offense to Shakespeare. This is the unmanifested absolute of spiritual traditions.

Silence allows for sound. Space allows for matter. Time allows for evolution. These are three forms of unfolding. Silence, space, and time have the interesting characteristic of being and not being simultaneously, no offense to Shakespeare. This is the unmanifested absolute of spiritual traditions.

What are we going to do concretely with these considerations that *seem* at first light-years away from our topic? We are going to change our perception of the universe. Just that. By starting at the top—the vision—we will have no trouble aligning the bottom—the practical application in everyday life.

This understanding allows us to define our priorities, which, aligned with universal principles, transcend our human and social priorities.

Space, silence, and time become luxuries. You come to pity those who can only live by trying to fill the void with objects, silence with sounds, or time with activities.

You perceive that everything that comes to fill this void is but a game, an illusion grafted onto your true nature. We are all actors, and this world is the stage. But the script belongs to us. The more you remember that you're at the heart of a cosmic play, the more freedom and latitude you have to shape the script.

Conversely, the more seriously you take the play, the more you attach to what *seems* to compose it, and the more you're chained to the pre-established and imposed scenario at your entrance on stage. And the more you suffer.

And what do you suffer from? From lack when you don't have and from the fear of losing when you do. The funny thing is, you already have everything. By drowning in accumulation and the race for "always more," you lose sight of this simple fact: you are *already* complete and perfect, lacking nothing. So enjoy life, use objects, speech, action but remain its master. Don't be a slave to what, in the end, only exists for the duration of a dream, on a midsummer's night.

Therapy through Emptiness or the Art of Contradiction

"Too many people spend money they haven't earned, to buy things they don't want, to impress people they don't like." - *Will Rogers*

We tend to think that we need to be well to get our life on track, improve our relationships, organize our affairs, and achieve our goals.

This is justified and partly true. But only partly. Indeed, another approach is possible, one that goes in the opposite direction and whose result is just as certain: the one that goes from the outside in.

In other words:

- Smiling will automatically produce, after a certain time, a feeling of joy and happiness;

- Appearing relaxed will produce relaxation;

- Throwing away, cleaning, and tidying will produce a feeling of clarity and inner peace.

What is crucial in life, what ultimately determines success or failure, is the feeling. One can succeed externally, but if one does not have the corresponding feeling of success, one cannot say that one has succeeded. Money, relationships, career, success, fame... none of this can be deemed a success without the feeling generally associated with it.

Similarly, we can experience these feelings without the material correspondences we think are necessary actually being present in our life. We can feel rich with the little we have. Happy regardless of conditions. At peace amidst turmoil and trials.

Does this make it a false happiness? A false peace? In other words, can a feeling be artificial and built on illusions? Of course not. A feeling, unlike an idea, does not lie. You can convince yourself that you believe in this or that concept, but you cannot cheat on what you feel.

And how do we evoke a feeling? By creating the conditions for its arrival. Often, we confuse the external state with the corresponding feeling. If you tell me that your dearest wish is to possess a certain sum, let's say a hundred thousand euros, I will ask you why.

For instance, it might be to feel more secure. What you are actually seeking, then, is not so much the money as the feeling of security you associate with that sum. If, therefore, I offered to provide you with this complete feeling, irrespective of actually receiving the money, you would probably accept. And you would be right, of course, because your goal would be achieved.

That's why decluttering and creating emptiness acts as therapy and brings you closer to your real goal, which is a feeling. The external and the internal are in some way intimately linked. While you cannot control everything that happens in your life, you can manage certain things as you wish, such as your health, which you can try to preserve by following healthy lifestyle rules, or your living environment.

This is the whole purpose of decluttering.

Freedom vs. Security

"Be less afraid, hope more; eat less, chew more; complain less, breathe more; talk less, say more; love more, and all the good things will be yours." - *Swedish Proverb*

The concept of freedom is often opposed to that of security. Philosophically speaking, this is justified. The commonly accepted feeling of security implies an underlying desire to maintain a certain status quo, to protect what belongs to us, to insure against the vicissitudes of life, to surround ourselves with possessions, to save.

However, security based on such premises, all external and subject to change or loss, can only ultimately be a source of anxiety and suffering.

In reality, true security is found in one place only: within oneself. If placed here, this feeling is intimately associated with that of freedom. It is no longer opposed to it, but one becomes the extension of the other. Being free provides an incredible sense of security. Feeling secure offers a fantastic sense of freedom.

But what prevents us from being free? Our attachments, of course. We are attached to everything: objects, people, memories, a place, prejudices, beliefs, the past, our addictions, everything we suppose defines our identity.

Decluttering, the gateway to minimalism, allows us to put all this into perspective. Getting rid of the material superfluous encourages us to do the same in all areas: relationships, professional life, schedules, hobbies...

Freedom is perhaps the most beautiful fruit, the quintessence of minimalism, its ultimate goal. You can surround yourself with possessions, castles, fill your bank accounts, take all possible insurances, and yet, you might not necessarily achieve this feeling. You'll be driven to protect your belongings, your image, your lifestyle.

In a minimalist life, there's nothing to protect. What truly matters is within us, always available. A burglar can come; they won't take away anything essential, even if they took everything.

And that's where freedom provides true security. We no longer try to protect what doesn't matter. We are free to move across the world overnight. We can give away the little we have and start over elsewhere.

We become more attentive, more present, more open, more available. Our values change and they change us. At this stage, we secretly make those envious who thought they owned everything and realize they are missing, and will always miss, something. They sense that what you possess, this inner peace, this joy, cannot be bought.

It only demands, and this is not a sacrifice, to give the first place, and gradually all the place, to what lies *behind* the material side of the world. To harmony, order, symmetry, right proportions, ecological awareness, valuing humanity.

This quest then becomes spiritual. Our inner and outer worlds harmonize and then merge into a coherent whole. And from this alchemy arises a great sense of security.

Then, we are free.

Part 2: ...and A Lot of Practice!

In this part, I'll share the fundamental principles of decluttering. Beyond specific situations or rooms, these are meant to be universal guidelines that you can apply in all circumstances. Numerous books delve into specifics: clothing, kitchen, books, bedroom... While useful, a good understanding of the principles beforehand will enable you to be independent, no matter the scenario.

I will, however, provide some practical examples.

Decluttering is not organizing the disorder

"One can very luxuriously furnish a room by unfurnishing it rather than furnishing it." - *Francis Jourdain*

When we start to declutter our homes, there's a phase almost everyone eventually faces. A confusing phase, a kind of in-between where we no longer want to live in the usual disorder but don't feel ready to throw things away yet.

At this stage, we often opt for a third, paradoxical way: organizing the disorder. Written down, this phrase might seem amusing, but in the moment, it feels like a fantastic idea. We might as well say: harmonizing the mess or ordering the chaos. We wouldn't be far from the truth.

Here, despite our intentions to clear our living space, the temptation is great to go *buy* all sorts of boxes, hangers, covers, cardboard, bags, etc. Initially pleased with ourselves, after a while we realize two things:

- we haven't eliminated anything
- we've added things to eliminate

At first glance, it might seem like a good idea to sort and meticulously organize those dozens of trinkets, screws, jewelry, perfume samples, paper clips, candles, photos, knick-knacks, pens, socks, in short, all that clutter that meticulously horrified us as it sprawled before our tired eyes. But in reality, *we've only shifted the problem.*

Because the problem does not stem from poor **organization** (though that exists and adds to the overall disorder) but from an **accumulation** that stifles our living space and our mind.

Therefore, don't lose sight of the essence, the philosophy behind decluttering: it's primarily and fundamentally about lightening up. Of course, it's preferable to live in a tidy apartment than in an unfathomable jumble, but the objective of a simplified, lightened, unburdened life is lost.

This goal itself bears many delightful fruits, but if you do not make the choice to truly rid yourself of everything that chains you, everything that keeps you attached to the past or to material possessions, you will not be able to access them.

Consequently, rather than tidying up, which most of the time amounts to *hiding* this or that item you don't really need, and if you can't bring yourself to throw it away, then *display it.*

Yes, exactly, let it sit there, on the living room table, prominently. After a while, two options will present themselves:

- either it is truly useful to you or dear to your heart, and its function is therefore to be always available or permanently displayed;

- or it is useless to you or you're not really attached to it, and its function is to leave your home. In this case, give it away.

It will surely be useful to someone who really needs it and cannot afford to buy it.

Every Day, One Less Item: Kaizen Applied to Decluttering

"We ascribe beauty to that which is simple; which has no superfluous parts; which exactly answers its end." - *Ralph Waldo Emerson*

It's a great joy and luxury, in our society that promotes excessive consumption and associates the idea of happiness with the number of possessions an individual has, to be able to say *every day*: today, I own less than yesterday. While everyone else dreams only of buying, accumulating, collecting, and each new day sees their homes invaded by new acquisitions they mostly don't really need, you, on the other hand, use it as an opportunity to free yourself. **One day at a time.**

Of course, it's just a habit, a routine to establish if you will. **This does not replace decluttering**. It's about accustoming your subconscious to the idea that throwing away or giving is a **normal** process. Thus, at the end of a year, without even noticing or feeling like you have made a sacrifice, you will have disposed of no less than 365 objects.

This is the principle of kaizen, or the method of small steps, which allows the accomplishment of great things that seemed impossible, one step at a time. With this method, you can do absolutely anything:

- Resume sports after a long break: start, for example, with *one* push-up or *one* abdominal exercise the first week, then two the next week, etc.

- Write a book: *one* page or even a minimum of *one* sentence each day, then let it flow if inspiration comes...

- Diet: eliminate *one* fry (if you eat them) the first day, two the second day, etc.

Applied to the subject at hand, this method acts as a constant subconscious reminder not to let oneself be overwhelmed and to resist the numerous solicitations from all kinds of merchants. In addition to this, it has the effect of forcing you to search and *find* what your interior, and therefore you, can do without.

It's not necessarily about immediately taking the item in question down to the trash. In fact, most of the time, that's to be avoided. Waste is never a good idea, especially if what you're looking to discard can still be of use. But in this case, you can plan to use a box that you'll place in a discreet spot (as long as you don't forget about it!), which you'll get rid of at the end of the week by donating or selling it. In the latter case, post the ad online the same day if possible and give yourself a week to dispose of it.

If no one has shown interest by then, it's either:

- because your price is not realistic (who wants to pay €500 for Great Aunt Berthe's old vase with the large patterns?);
- or... it's simply not interesting.

Remember, we live in a time when you can easily and often inexpensively find almost anything you want.

Don't underestimate the intelligence of your potential customers when you post your ads.

It will be beneficial for them, and for you as well.

Gather to See and Touch

"Beware of any enterprise that requires new clothes." - *Henry David Thoreau*

Take a tour of your apartment and gather all the items belonging to the category you've decided to tackle, such as clothes, then group them in the living room, directly on the floor (which you will have cleaned beforehand, obviously).

Try to also bring in those that are in the laundry basket. Leave aside only those that are drying and, of course, those you are wearing. Think about shoes, coats, scarves, hats...

If you've never done this before, you'll be astonished. Not only will you wonder how you could have amassed so many clothes, but for some, you won't even know why they are there or where they came from.

Before moving on to the practical step, let's answer the question: why gather everything like this?

Well! Having in front of you what you own should indeed... open your eyes, in addition to answering that question. We do not suspect the extent of our possessions, in this case, our *clutter* (there's no other word) until we see it as it is, laid out in front of us. Like Saint Thomas, we cannot believe it until we have seen it.

This sudden awareness is a powerful engine for action. This works with all categories of objects, of course: dishes, care and beauty products, books and cultural products, various supplies, knick-knacks...

But why spread everything *on the floor*? Because after making a choice (to discard or keep), everything will need to be organized properly! This will make you hesitate about the usefulness of keeping that old pilled sweater or the 22-volume encyclopedia full of dust.

But seeing is not enough. Take each object in hand, touch it, or even smell it, and ask yourself this simple question: does this still have a role to play in my life? Does this garment make me happy? Does this knick-knack cheer up my view? Does this book still bring me joy?

Only you can answer these questions. However, as we will see later, your goal is to limit yourself to a certain number of items in your home, across all categories.

Therefore, what you save on care creams will have repercussions on the dishes and vice versa. This exercise allows for an equitable distribution of what you own.

Setting limits allows us to define our so-called "vital needs" and not give in to all our whims.

Remember, without some discipline, your old habits, coupled with the pressure of social norms, will quickly bring you back to square one.

If you truly want to break free from the past and make room for the new in your life, you need to take radical measures and know how to make cuts. This cannot be done while pitying yourself over the first piece of rag you come across.

An Example: High-Tech Devices

"Life is really simple, but we insist on making it complicated." - *Confucius*

There was a time when I had in my living room: an amplifier, a CD player, a gaming console and its controllers, a DVD player, speakers, a television, a computer (tower + monitor + keyboard + mouse), a printer, an internet router, plus of course the furniture to hold all this (a large TV stand, speaker stands, a desk for the PC) and the countless cables and wires of all kinds to connect everything.

Obviously, to operate these various devices, add to this CDs, DVDs, games, software, and the furniture to store them.

Today, I've replaced all that clutter with a laptop and a quality Bluetooth speaker.

I've kept an LCD TV that I've mounted on the wall but did it more for my children than for myself. No doubt I'll get rid of it without difficulty when the time comes.

No more cables lying everywhere (no matter how much you try to hide them, they're always visible), no more power strips plugged into other power strips, no manuals, warranties to keep, objects to dust, bulky furniture.

Today, you can find almost everything you want on the internet: music, movies, games, information, books, magazines, photos, recipes, guides...

This era, regardless of the criticisms that can be made of it, offers us tremendous possibilities in terms of dematerialization and all the advantages that come with it: saving the planet's resources, no need to store a myriad of objects at home, easy sharing with loved ones or even the entire world. Why deprive ourselves?

I still remember the times when, traveling to visit distant relatives, I had to include in my luggage a whole collection of CDs to listen to music during the journey. If I had some photos to show, I needed to bring albums. I always planned on bringing multiple books, just "in case." In short, I weighed myself down.

Today, an ultra-light laptop and possibly a USB drive are all it takes to bring everything with you. And even if you leave without these, if your host has a computer, you can easily show them your latest vacation snaps that you've put in the *cloud*, this computer cloud that allows you to store almost anything you want on remote computer servers via the internet.

Moreover, by properly configuring your smartphone, which for most of us also serves as a camera, the transfer to the cloud is done automatically.

The "boxes" from internet service providers, which are essential, are on their way to becoming more compact, and most offer all-in-one models today.

The only cables that should be allowed in your home are the power cables. No doubt one day we will find a technology that allows us to transport electrical current wirelessly, or even power devices differently. Alas, that's not yet possible today.

However, even in the current state, freeing oneself from all these objects has become very easy. The gain, in terms of space as well as practicality, is undeniable. Don't deprive yourself of it.

This little chapter might make people smile a few years from now when the devices it describes as modern will be obsolete, but for the moment it's the current state of our technology. If there are still readers by then, let them consider this part as a testimony!

Children

"That's all well and good, but the people writing these books on minimalism don't have kids!" - *some parents*

False.

I know because I have them myself, three boys, who are currently teenagers to boot. And everything is going very well.

The important thing is to define everyone's boundaries. A child is entitled to their private space. I don't take care of decluttering their rooms. At most, I make suggestions or remarks. My only requirement is hygiene, which is also part of education.

As for common areas, everyone is asked to tidy up after themselves, leave places clean, and not to leave everything and anything in their wake. None of this is really demanding.

Moreover, living in a clear and simple environment instills in them a certain notion of order, harmony, and simplicity, which will affect their well-being and peace. This setting is favorable for both studies and leisure.

And video games? Indeed, nowadays, whether we like it or not, children, especially boys, play these games. So what to do?

For my part, I've opted for the following solution: my children are allowed to have a computer in their room, which they can tinker with as they wish. I monitor the time they spend on it, that's all.

To give you an example of how one might try to reason when looking for the simplest solution and the maximum utility value of an object or device, let's take a moment to consider the case of the computer.

The advantages of a computer over a gaming console are clear:

- First, it's multi-tasking: on a PC, you can play games, surf the web, study, write, learn, chat, share on social networks, watch movies, listen to music. A console is primarily for playing games.

- Next, its upgradeable nature means you can physically update it as technology advances, which is also very educational in terms of understanding how a machine works. A console becomes obsolete quickly.

- Finally, and to keep it brief, the power of a PC far exceeds that of a console and easily allows for network gaming, even within the home. Some even predict the imminent demise of physical consoles, foreseeing game access through the *cloud*.

You can apply this reasoning to any object by listing the advantages and disadvantages of owning one thing over another, or simply of owning it.

For everything related to clothes and personal belongings, everyone is encouraged to keep their room tidy. In the bathroom, everyone has their toiletry bag.

Teaching your child to tidy up and clean up after themselves is, of course, a great thing. It teaches them respect and independence, in addition to giving them good reflexes that will serve them all their life. It's not about making them obsessive: it's about making them careful, which is very different.

It's about teaching them to take care of what they own as well as their environment, and providing them, through example, with an ideal framework for development and well-being.

It's gently guiding them towards maturity.

How Many Items Should You Own at Home?

"Wealth consists not in having great possessions, but in having few wants." - *Aristote*

How many items do you need to live well? It's hard to give a precise answer to this question because each person is different. What matters is not so much the number but the actual utility or pleasure one derives from them.

However, to set a benchmark, you might find it interesting to list the 100 items you would keep in your home if you had to. Such lists can be found on the internet or in certain books. You can use these as a starting point and adapt them to your needs and tastes.

As we've seen before, there's no need to accumulate a multitude of items in the same category.

For example, with dishes, there's no need to have 12 plates, 10 bowls, 6 water glasses plus 6 wine glasses, 3 oven-safe dishes, etc., if you live alone. Adjust your dishware to the number of people in the household.

If you're organizing a party, which is by definition exceptional, it will always be possible to borrow what you lack.

I personally opted for the number six, first because most sets are sold this way, and secondly because this number amply suffices for me.

I don't have differentiated glasses. In the past, partly to impress, I owned water glasses, wine glasses, Champagne flutes, Martini glasses, beer glasses... Almost one glass per drink! Today, my single set of six glasses serves for everything, and the taste remains the same.

I favor containers that can be used for multiple purposes, such as bowls. Not only can they hold meals (a very common practice in Japan), but they can also replace soup plates for soups and stews.

For clothes (a sensitive subject for many women), the reasoning is the same. Set yourself a fixed and limited number of outfits. Organize complete outfits to help you, one for each day of the week, plus one or two for occasional events.

Prefer versatile clothing, such as suits that can be suitable for daily use as well as for more chic events. For men, a mismatched trouser-jacket ensemble can work well if you don't wear a suit on a daily basis.

In general, try to equip yourself with multifunctional objects or appliances. Don't unnecessarily accumulate multiple items that will require maintenance and expenses.

Try to think in numbers, setting a limit for each category, with a total threshold not to exceed, which you will determine based on your actual needs.

Many people manage very well with a hundred items. If they can do it, so can you. It may seem like a small number, but the trade-off is living in a healthy, uncluttered, clean space, where you know and precisely appreciate the value of the few things you own.

And that's worth all the possessions in the world.

Additional Questions, Techniques, and Tips

"One of the heaviest chains to carry is that of material possessions." - *Constantin Zuraïo*

The following questions aim to make you aware of the real value you attribute to what you own:

- Imagine a fire ravaging your home. Which possessions would you truly regret losing?

- If you had to evacuate your home urgently, what would you spontaneously take with you?

- If you had to leave with nothing but a knapsack, what would you fill it with?

- If you had to move and lighten your load as much as possible, how would you go about it?

- A TV crew is coming in an hour to film every corner of your home for a live broadcast on a show about decoration and organization. Panic on board?

- What would you refuse to sell regardless of the price offered?

- Among everything you own, what would you like to pass on to your children?

- If everything behind a closed door (closet, wardrobe, pantry) was visible, would your home suddenly become a real clutter?

- Do you keep things because they were given to you?

Aside from the previously mentioned exercises, like gathering and touching, here are some tips that should help you progress on the path to decluttering:

- Make a list of everything you own. If you can't, it means there are too many things in your home. Then, subdivide by rooms.

- Sort the listed items by size, from the most cumbersome to the smallest. Could you replace the bulky items with something more streamlined, or even do without them?

- Do you have duplicate items for the same purpose? In that case, decide which one to keep and say goodbye to the other.

- Search the internet for photos of minimalist apartments or houses. Choose one that you really like, a setting where you could see yourself living, and set it as your wallpaper.

- If you have items that you believe are valuable, check their value on sites like eBay. If they are indeed valuable, it might be worth selling them. Otherwise, you won't have too much trouble getting rid of them.

- For one week, remove all the knick-knacks cluttering your shelves and furniture and store them in a box. Then, see how you feel at the end of this period. The same or better? Don't put them back, give them away.

- You can do the same exercise with frames and paintings decorating your walls.

- Clear all flat surfaces of everything they contain and then wipe them down. Leave them empty.

- Choose ONE and only one decorative item for the living room, like a slender vase with a flower or a photo frame. Instead of being drowned out by a multitude of objects, it will be highlighted as it deserves.

- Identify anything in your home that is cracked, chipped, moth-eaten, holed, broken, or deformed, and throw it away.

These techniques will help you keep your interior uncluttered and impeccable. Revisit them regularly and feel free to add your own notes, what works for you.

Part 3: Going Further

While philosophy underpins a good integration of minimalism into one's life, and a few techniques are sufficient for its concrete application, exploring some parallel paths that have a direct connection with our topic can be enriching.

The following themes offer avenues for reflection that align with a life based on independence, a return to essential values, or the pitfalls one may encounter along the way.

Freeing Yourself from the Tyranny of Commerce

"To try to satisfy desires by acquiring possessions is like trying to extinguish a fire with straw." - *Chinese Proverb*

It's hard for us to imagine today that there was a time when one could walk around without seeing an advertisement, watch a sports competition without our field of vision being invaded by brand names, or watch a movie without multiple interruptions.

Welcome to the world of commercial tyranny.

Whether we lament it or not, unless we choose to live in self-sufficiency in the countryside, we are constantly subjected to it. However, we are free to succumb to it or not, and we can implement strategies to avoid being overwhelmed by all this propaganda.

In this world of fierce competition, wild relocations, depletion of resources, planned obsolescence, in short, in this economic jungle, all means are fair for survival.

What interest would a company have in manufacturing a product that lasts a lifetime? That's why fashion and marketing exist. Sometimes, real technological evolutions emerge that genuinely meet a need and change the game, but often the arguments for changing and renewing your possessions are just pure marketing tactics.

"This winter, the trend is pink," "this season, you need an LED panel screen," "this new yogurt will replenish the bacteria in your stomach"... The list is endless of the indispensable novelties you must absolutely own. Against this system, one simple solution: **a list of basics**.

Good products that have stood the test of time, reliable values, timeless items. For categories of recent products that don't fit this mold, define your needs. Do you really need a printer-scanner-copier if you only use it occasionally? Consider the space such a machine occupies.

Do you absolutely need the latest coffee maker and its expensive individual capsules (after all, the fees for the celebrities who endorse them have to come from somewhere)? I personally have a small Italian coffee maker that brews coffee with an unmatched aroma, never breaks down, and even lets me forego a filter. *What else?*

Thus, it's essential to define your needs.

No one knows better than you what suits you or not. No one knows you better than yourself.

The key is not to let yourself be trapped anymore. Generally speaking, anyone who flatters you has an interest in doing so. *"Because you're worth it"*...

But you know your own worth. You don't need someone else, who moreover doesn't know you, to tell you.

Gradually, you'll realize that your choices will come from within yourself, and ultimately will only be dictated by you *first and foremost*. Does this make you selfish? You know it does not.

Selfishness is thinking only of oneself, even to the detriment of others. Making life choices, which is a right, is not the same.

Moreover, this approach, which is also motivated by an awareness of the scarcity of planetary resources, is clearly an altruistic choice that considers both contemporaries and future generations.

Rediscover the Taste of "Homemade"

"The simplest things are often the truest." - *Richard Bach*

Prepared meals, pre-squeezed juices... Nowadays, the trend is towards the prefabricated. No need to bother, someone has done it for you. No need to make an effort, it's taken care of for you.

While the idea may seem appealing at first, it carries its own downside: it clips your wings and gradually numbs your ability to be autonomous and independent.

You come to expect the work to be done for you and find this normal.

Like any skill, the one that involves managing on your own strengthens if you use it and weakens if you don't.

Of course, buying ready-to-assemble furniture can be justified. Unless you have the necessary know-how, you're not going to make your own furniture.

The same goes for ready-to-wear; not everyone can make their own clothes.

However, for more basic tasks, it's a shame to sacrifice your skills and creativity for something pre-formatted.

The underlying idea is that someone else - usually a company - will do it better than you.

But are you sure that a major soup brand will do better than you if you give it a try? Your mother or grandmother could very well teach you a few tricks and family secrets, and if you don't have them, the internet is full of recipes for homemade and delicious soups. And it only takes tasting and comparing a packet soup and a homemade soup once to know which is better. This, of course, applies to all dishes.

What the industry really sells you is not expertise but time-saving.

Are you sure you want to trade quality, good taste, and authenticity to save a bit of time? And especially to do what? A little more internet surfing? Not to miss the start of a reality TV show?

Of course, my point is not to judge anyone's interests or priorities. But I believe that if you're reading this book, you've already realized the futility of this mode of reasoning, which is more often the result of habit than a genuine internal deliberation.

Taking the time to do things yourself, whether it's cooking a good meal, a household chore, making a piece of clothing, a painting, or anything else, according to your inclinations and abilities, provides a pleasure incomparable to buying a ready-made, soulless, and often tasteless product.

In the final analysis, being and having, while not absolutely opposed, respond to two different logics and do not provide the same pleasure. While the end goal of the process remains the same (eating, observing, using...), the process leading up to it is just as important as the outcome.

Of course, you're not going to build the components of a computer yourself (but you can assemble it if you need a desktop PC), perform an appendectomy, or construct a building if you lack the skills.

But for the small, everyday things, from cooking to cleaning to gardening, you already have everything you need to please yourself and others, gain autonomy, and improve the quality of whatever you decide to undertake.

Because what you do yourself corresponds to you, in addition to allowing you to discover a bit more about yourself each time.

Who can do it better than you?

Not Re-cluttering

"Have nothing in your houses that you do not know to be useful or believe to be beautiful." - *William Morris*

After successfully decluttering your home and beginning to appreciate the results, many people go through a strange phase after some time: the temptation to refill that dearly won space.

Like any new habit we adopt, we need a period of adjustment, and this is where vigilance is required. While we were motivated to declutter, we suddenly begin to doubt the soundness of our choice. While we were arguing in favor of minimalism, we no longer really know what drove us to try it.

We want to return to our previous state, which, although it did not bring us particular satisfaction, had the advantage of being familiar to us. In short, we doubt.

When this phase hits you, if it does, recognize it for what it is: *a reflex of fear*.

Fear of the new, fear of emptiness, fear of non-conformity, fear of what others will say, fear of freedom... The list of all the fears associated with getting rid of material things is long.

Many people are terrified by the ideas of emptiness, space, silence, solitude, retreat. They desperately fill their homes, their schedules, their address books, their stomachs, their beds, their mp3 players, everything they can, all the time, to not risk being alone... with themselves.

Behind this fear, for at its core there's only one in many forms, lie deep metaphysical causes whose analysis would exceed the scope of this book.

However, it's enough for you to know that this reflex to regress is *normal* and that there's no need to feel guilty.

When it occurs, *be patient*.

Don't deny yourself anything, mentally allow yourself the possibility of going back whenever you please, but wait a bit. Resist the temptation to rush into stores or to order all sorts of things online.

Wait a few days and, rather than staying locked up at home, *go out*.

If possible, visit some friends whom you know live in particularly cluttered and disorganized homes. If you're like me, this shouldn't be too hard to find!

When you return home in the evening, the contrast will hit you in the face, and you'll appreciate even more all the efforts you've made to get there.

If you manage to weather this storm that pushes you to regress (and you will!), you'll realize, once calm returns, how right you were both to embark on this process and to resist the temptation to give it up.

This time, you'll be serene, definitively. You'll no longer envy the cluttered interiors of your family or friends, you'll no longer doubt the relevance of your choices, and you'll have gained confidence in yourself and your ability to think for yourself, outside the norms.

Unplug!

"Simplicity is the ultimate sophistication." - *Leonardo da Vinci*

Sometimes, to counterbalance the multitude of solicitations we are constantly subject to, it's beneficial to be able to isolate ourselves, to preserve ourselves. Even in the heart of big cities, there's a simple way to do this: unplug.

Television, internet, phone, social media... we tend to forget, but there's a simple way not to be constantly solicited by these various time-consuming tools. Leave them off and don't check them.

Regarding television and the internet, it's relatively simple since their use depends solely on your will.

For the phone and social media, however, it might seem difficult to cut off since other people may need to reach you and could worry about your silence.

In this case, the simplest solution is to inform your circle: you won't be reachable for one, two, three days, or more, as you prefer. It's a bit like you're going abroad to a secluded spot where no network is accessible.

Don't worry, the Earth won't stop spinning, and it's highly unlikely that an absolute emergency will occur. After all, how did our parents and grandparents manage?

Some people are so "addicted" to social media these days that this area is now officially considered a new addictive behavior, just like drugs. The fear of missing out on something important on social media (FOMO) is a good example.

To avoid falling into such extremes, it's good (and recommended) to take regular breaks, in other words: to unplug.

Unplugging isn't necessarily about cutting off from electronic means of communication.

It could be taking time for oneself instead of joining friends at the pub where you regularly go (which also helps you avoid drinking too much alcohol), doing a fast or a diet, taking a break from your habits, leaving work at reasonable hours...

The idea is to take a break, to isolate oneself temporarily to better find oneself, to take time to reflect on oneself, one's life, one's projects.

Take a *real* weekend off and go somewhere you don't know and where nobody knows you. Take long walks, breathe in different and, if possible, purer air, clear your mind of daily worries. In short, rejuvenate.

You'll come back in great shape, with new creative ideas. You'll have a clearer vision of the meaning of your life and the direction you want to give it.

Unplugging from the daily grind is actually, at the same time, reconnecting with our inner source, from where only true ideas can spring, those with the capacity to change our life.

By isolating yourself in appearance, you're in fact connecting to a current of energy, to a flow of consciousness that has the ability to bring you everything that really matters in life, in addition to helping you solve your problems more effectively.

Peace of heart, happiness, well-being cannot be bought. They are the fruits we reap when we make space within ourselves and get rid of the old to sow the seeds of the new.

With a little patience, the harvest will be glorious.

Epilogue: The Bare Life

"What the caterpillar calls the end, the butterfly calls the beginning." - *Violette Lebon*

The simple life, the bare life... these two expressions resonate innately. Why? Because we arrive naked into this world, and we leave just as naked.

Does this mean we are devoid of anything? Not at all!

For we arrive on Earth with the essential: the energy of life.

And we leave with the essential: our experiences.

And what will really have mattered in between, when the time comes to leave this world?

Not what you will have accumulated, collected, hoarded. Even though leaving a material legacy for your descendants can help them in life, it's not the most important thing, nor what they will remember you by.

What you will leave behind is the love you managed to give. It's what you were able to offer, whether it be a smile, advice, or a meal made with love. You will never be loved for your money if that's all you have to offer.

Life must be shared, like joy, creativity, the talents with which we are endowed.

All these qualities, by definition immaterial, are alive. They don't gather dust, are indestructible and eternal, are always available, and belong to each and everyone.

What's the point of hanging dozens of masterpieces on your walls if the canvas inside you never got to emerge? What's the use of collecting old vinyls if you never let your inner music express itself?

What do you need these soulless objects for? Will they replace yours? Will they allow you to express your joy and spread your desire for life?

And aren't you *unique*? So why settle for admiring the uniqueness of others?

Share yours. Offer it to the world as a gift, regardless of whether it touches one person or a million.

You've been given life as a gift, pay it forward by expressing yourself and sharing who you are. Don't underestimate yourself. What you have to offer can only be offered by you.

So instead of letting yourself be suffocated by the material world and the trivialities that dream merchants dangle before your eyes, prioritize life and its expression.

This is what decluttering and minimalism lead us to: through the progressive stripping away of all that doesn't matter, what really matters is revealed.

Like a sculptor who brings out a timeless masterpiece from raw stone by gradually removing what covered it, which only he could see in his mind, you can make your life a masterpiece by removing everything that covers the treasure you have to offer.

Finding yourself in a simple, harmonious environment full of space will provide the setting that allows you to express what you carry within: life, which needs nothing to *be*.

The bare life.

Printed in Great Britain
by Amazon

45030839R00046